620

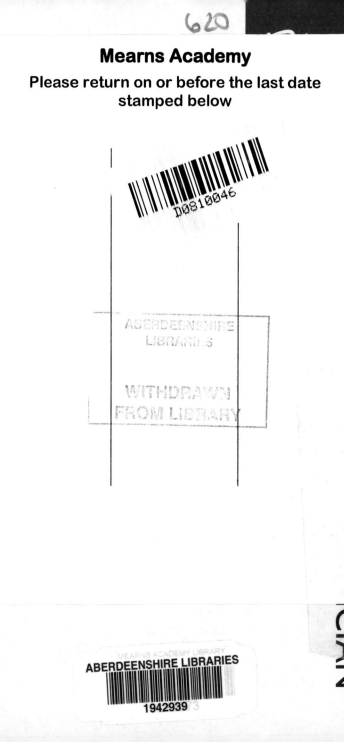

Mearns Academy

Please return on or before the last date stamped below

REAL LIFE GUIDES

Practical guides for practical people

In this series of career guides from Trotman, we look in detail at what it takes to train for, get into and be successful at a wide spectrum of practical careers. The *Real Life Guides* aim to inform and inspire young people and adults alike by providing comprehensive yet hard-hitting and often blunt information about what it takes to succeed in these careers.

Other titles in this series are:

trotman

Real
Life
GUIDES

ENGINEERING TECHNICIAN

Neil Harris

Real Life Guides: Engineering Technician
This first edition published in 2008 by Trotman Publishing,
a division of Crimson Publishing Ltd., Westminster House,
Kew Road, Richmond, Surrey TW9 2ND

© Trotman Publishing 2008

Author Neil Harris

British Library Cataloguing in Publication Data
A catalogue record for this book is available from the British
Library

ISBN 978 1 84455 169 9

Typeset by RefineCatch Ltd, Bungay, Suffolk

Printed and bound in Great Britain by Athenaeum Press,
Gateshead

Real
Life

GUIDES

CONTENTS

About the author

Dr Neil Harris started his career in engineering, working with a manufacturer of metals and then with a turbine manufacturer. Changing career he became a career counsellor and Director of the Careers Services at Imperial College, Kings College London and UCL. Now director of Lifelines Personal Development Ltd in St Albans he writes about careers and offers careers advice.

Acknowledgements

Thanks to my wife Daphne for her encouragement. Thanks also to Viv Turner of The Learning and Skills Council, Rita Congera of the Institution of Mechanical Engineers and Alison Riley of the Institution of Engineering and Technology for their invaluable assistance.

Foreword

Not everyone sees their future in an office environment; if you're very 'hands-on' then working within engineering can be exceptionally rewarding and exciting. The employment opportunities within engineering are varied and the industry has undergone significant change in recent times, diversifying in order to compete with robust international competition. As a result new opportunities have emerged allowing for jobs that are based less on traditional engineering skills and more on technological and green engineering. Some of this is the direct result of governmental policies such as climate change issues and improvements in transportation infrastructure. These areas have grown in size and status ensuring a positive picture for the future of the industry.

City & Guilds works closely with sector skills councils to make sure all our engineering qualifications meet industry requirements. Our working relationships with industry leaders allow us to deliver some of the most up-to-date, relevant and flexible qualifications which suit learners of all levels, with high levels of recognition from employers in the UK, as well as internationally.

Our qualifications support learners from pre-entry to employment, including apprenticeships, with progression right through to management, professional or further education. Some of our major qualifications, which form part of the apprenticeship framework, include NVQs in Performing Engineering Operations, Aeronautical Engineering and Computer Aided Design. We also offer vocationally related qualifications (VRQs) which develop knowledge and understanding, can assist with entry and progression, and form the technical certificate within the apprenticeship.

City & Guilds is delighted to be part of the Trotman *Real Life Guides* series to help raise your awareness of these vocational qualifications. If a job in engineering appeals to you then City & Guilds have qualifications which will support your development throughout your career, helping you to achieve excellence and quality in whichever field you choose. So for more information about the courses City & Guilds offer check out www.cityandguilds.com and you could end up designing parts for one of the biggest aerospace companies in Europe.

Peter Maskell
Business Support Manager
City & Guilds

Introduction

Are you a practical person? Do you enjoy making things; taking things apart, tinkering and putting them back together again? Have you ever made model aeroplanes or something similar? Do you enjoy working with your hands on things you can see and touch rather than imagining ideas in your head or getting into things you don't see which may not seem as useful, like computer programs or financial accounts? Would you like to leave school or college and start a career in which you get trained and earn a living straight away instead of increasing your debts by continuing in full-time education?

If you answer yes to most questions like these, starting your career as an engineering technician is definitely worth considering. It's a career that has many advantages. First, you can do it in most places. Some jobs, like sailor, power station engineer or astronomer cannot be done everywhere, but all towns and cities have engineering technicians and they also work in the countryside. If you have itchy feet and want to travel the world you will have skills as an engineering technician that can be valuable in most places.

Next, and just as important, you can be an engineering technician in many different industries (Chapter 4). There are engineering technicians in electronics, aerospace, the armed forces, transport, power generation and distribution, shipping, schools and universities, car manufacturing, construction, food and chemicals and many other sectors. So you can choose the kind of organisation you work in to suit your circumstances, your interests and personality.

In this book we show you how to become an engineering technician (Chapter 7) and what the training involves. We investigate the key industries that employ technicians and look into what you would be doing if you worked there. There is an interview with Alec Osborn (Chapter 1), who started his career training to be an Engineering Technician in Formula 1 cars and rose to become the President of the Institution of Mechanical Engineers.

In Chapter 5 we explore the skills you require, the tools of the trade, to be successful in this career and in Chapter 6 we answer questions that are frequently asked by people who are considering making a start in this exciting profession. Chapter 3 provides examples of people who are doing the job now, have completed their training and work as engineering technicians. They have their own stories to tell and reading what they say you can see for yourself whether this is something you would like to do.

You might assume that it's a career for men, because in the past it was, but you would be wrong. It's a job for both sexes. As we will see later in this book, there are many women who take it up as a career and are successful, though it's true that they are still in the minority.

Another advantage is that there are many different types of engineering technician. Engineering is a vast subject and you can specialise in a range of areas, from telecommunications to mechanics, electrical engineering to chemical and food manufacture, defence to oil, gas and water. In each sector there is a special knowledge, which you can learn, that is slightly different to what an engineering technician would know and do in other parts of engineering.

If you choose this career you will, of course, have to train and learn all the techniques which you will apply in practice but training is readily available (Chapter 7). A key attraction of this career is that it is definitely not a dead end. You can, if you wish, progress to more senior roles later in your career, gaining experience and qualifications along the way. This is a career where you set the ceiling of your achievement, not someone else. People like Alan Sugar started in garages making and mending things and progressed to be among the most successful people of their generation.

Which brings us on to the possibility of being self-employed. Many engineering technicians work for themselves providing a service for their customers. It is quite possible, once you have mastered the engineering skills to apply them to things people want, such as mending computers or electrical equipment, making gadgets, repairing vehicles. Then you could be the boss and run your own business (Chapter 3, 'Real lives').

So what is an engineering technician? The Engineering Council, which oversees the engineering professions in the UK, says that engineering technicians are involved in 'applying proven techniques and procedures to the solution of practical engineering problems'. They 'exercise their creative aptitudes within their field of technology and

> ## DID YOU KNOW?
>
> With the initials EngTech after your name you have a 'valuable, portable, internationally recognised qualification protected by Royal Charter. Only registered Engineering Technicians can call themselves EngTech'.
>
> Source: The Engineering Council

contribute to the design, development, manufacture, commissioning, operation or maintenance of equipment, processes, or services'.

What does this mean? It means that as an engineering technician you will be applying your skills to practical engineering problems. These occur in many different ways. You could be building prototypes following a new design or testing out some fresh piece of equipment. You might be involved in a manufacturing process such as assembling cars on a production line or putting together a piece of electrical equipment. Alternatively you could be making parts that, when assembled together, make up a product. Most new products have to be tested before they leave the factory. Your job could include testing what has been made to be sure that it is safe, complies with the regulations and is in line with the drawings.

ALEC OSBORN

Success story

PRESIDENT OF THE IME AND CHIEF ENGINEER AT PERKINS ENGINES

Alec Osborn started his career as an Apprentice Engineering Technician and rose to become President of the Institution of Mechanical Engineers and Chief Engineer at Perkins Engines. The Queen appointed him an MBE. How did he do it?

'I came from a farming family,' says Alec, 'but my obsession was with aeroplanes, cars and railways and I was never really interested in agriculture. As a child I used to build things using "Meccano" and machinery on the farm satisfied my curiosity for mechanics.

'School was a disappointment for me. There were too many changes of school and a poor quality of teaching. However, I did pick up significant O levels (GCSE equivalents) in Maths, Physics and English. That was enough to get me an

My appren-
ticeship was
five years
of invaluable
training in a
high profile
environment
and I was
engrossed in
my interest
of engines
and cars.

apprenticeship at Rubery Owen Ltd, then the largest privately owned engineering firm in the UK, a place on an ONC course and escaped from school when I was 16 years old.

'I had a lot of catching up to do if I was going to achieve my ambitions. I was posted to the engine development division, then known as British Racing Motors (BRM) which got me into the Formula 1 car racing environment. I had a fantastic year as a mechanic member of the racing team. I remember the scream of a Formula 1 engine, the delightful whiff of Castrol R and the tension of being on the starting grid for the races. We won the Grand Prix at Zandvoot. There was a lot of emotion behind our achievements. I was exposed to a high pressure situation with famous and capable people, which was good for my career.

'My apprenticeship was five years of invaluable training in a high profile environment and I was engrossed in my interest of engines and cars. I learnt all the practical engineering skills of turning and fitting, milling and welding. Then I spent the last year of my apprenticeship in the drawing office.

'Meanwhile I was studying hard on day release, spending a day a week at college and attending evening classes. It was exhausting but it developed my tenacity and determination. I completed my Ordinary National Certificate and at that time I was offered the chance to take an engineering degree but I felt that it would be more valuable to gain practical engineering experience and study instead for an HNC. At that time few engineers took degrees. So I studied both production engineering and mechanical engineering at Grantham College of Further Education and finally got two

HNCs. It was an almost impossible task spending one day and three evenings a week at college. But it was good to be able to apply my knowledge back at the factory where I could put into practice what I had learnt.

'My apprenticeship completed, together with two HNCs, I set to work as a design engineer. My first full design was a new 1,000 cc Formula 2 engine for which I was presented with a prize from the Institution of Mechanical Engineers. It was my first experience of my professional body and it was a good one.

'There were more experiences with the design of Formula 1 engines, with plenty of novel concepts and feasibility projects. Then I did a complete change and moved into chassis design. It involved work on the suspension, track testing and race engineering. Using a wind tunnel to test the aerodynamics, we had a breakthrough with what became known as the "wing car". The principles of this novel idea eventually appeared in the Lotus 78 Formula 1 car. Motor racing gave me everything a young engineer could wish for. It introduced me to the high standards of mechanical engineering, a structured approach to problem solving and matured me as an engineer.

'I needed to broaden my experience into a production environment and at 30 years old I got the opportunity to join Perkins Engines in Peterborough as a Design Engineer working on diesel engines. It meant moving from a close knit team of 100 engineers to a factory producing 1,000 diesel engines a day and employing 9,000 people. I started as a Senior Design Engineer, designing many different types of engine from those on a vineyard tractor to those in battle tanks. There were a great variety of shapes and sizes for many different applications.

'A series of promotions followed including to Chief Engineer for Worldwide Applications, then Chief Engineer for Test Operations. Finally I became Head of all Product Design and Development, responsible for new engine programmes and upgrades of existing products.

'The highlight of my career was to be elected President of the Institution of Mechanical Engineers in 2006 having held a number of responsible chairman positions. In 2005 I was honoured to receive an MBE in the New Year honours list for services to education.

'My experience demonstrates that even if you have an unfortunate school experience you can get to the top of the tree. An apprenticeship gives you maturity, sound judgement and perspective together with an insight into how to handle numerous situations with people.

'There is currently a severe shortage of engineering technicians, a key job which can be the beginning of a rewarding career in engineering up to the highest level. I firmly believe that engineering continues to offer young people a rewarding career.

'My advice to all young engineers is:

- Individual success is dependent on many factors ranging from common sense to a determination to succeed.
- Excel at communicating and develop a broad understanding of the issues that confront you and your colleagues.

- Make an impact with what you do and say.
- Always establish the root cause of problems; this is far more productive than instinctively allocating blame.
- Be adventurous, but always learn from your mistakes.
- Recognise the power of teamwork as an achieving and motivational means of working.
- Avoid endless debate about titles and status. Satisfaction is in what you achieve and the responsibility that goes with it.
- Fight that little bit harder for what you aspire to be. Success is about self-belief, focus and determination.
- Integrity is paramount in engineering – the responsibility on your shoulders is huge.'

2

What's the story?

In this chapter we explore the many different industries in which you can work as an engineering technician and in Chapter 4 we discuss what you would actually be doing if you worked in them.

Everything that is man made has been engineered. That is most things we see around us. The Egyptians engineered the pyramids and the Romans built roads, baths and under-floor central heating systems called hypocausts, so engineering goes back a long way. They moved water around on aqueducts and used canals to transport goods.

Today we would call that civil engineering and construction is much more sophisticated now. It includes building motorways and bridges, tunnels and railways, skyscrapers and houses. Engineering technicians are involved as electricians, plumbers and in providing such services as telephones, heating, ventilating and refrigeration.

VEHICLES
Modern engineering has its roots in the nineteenth century with lots of inventions including the steam engine, the internal combustion engine, the light bulb and the telephone. Stephenson's Rocket, the first steam locomotive that provided transport, was only invented in the 1820s. Our modern transport system derives from there and offers

plenty of career opportunities. Now it's a huge business including ships, motor vehicles, aeroplanes and all the facilities that they need – docks, motorways, airports and navigation systems. Previously, manufacturing had been done by hand or using windmills but the engine and distributed electricity gave rise to the industrial revolution and factories with mass production of goods.

As an engineering technician you can be involved in mechanical, electrical, electronic and many other roles in what is now a vast industry. There are jobs in producing vehicles of all kinds, repairing them and helping motorists, plus the more glamorous side which is motor racing. Of course, there is much more to the automotive trade than cars and motor bikes. It includes vans, lorries and heavy goods vehicles, buses, tractors, agricultural machinery and all manner of vehicles. With around 32 million vehicles on the road in the UK, that adds up to plenty of work. Manufacturers include Ford, Vauxhall, Nissan, Toyota, Honda and Renault.

> **DID YOU KNOW?**
>
> The Institute for the Motor Industry is the key professional body and skills council for technicians working in car servicing and maintenance and servicing.

AEROSPACE

After Stephenson's Rocket, it took another 80 years, to 1900, for the Wright Brothers to build the first plane that could fly. It was powered by an internal combustion engine, a far cry from the modern jet. But there began the huge industry we now call aerospace, which includes not just aeroplanes for civil transport and defence but also private planes, rockets, satellites and space exploration. The modern aerospace industry is massive. It includes airlines and air forces, manufacturers such as Airbus and BAE Systems plus numerous organisations that supply the industry with parts. Firms such as Rolls-Royce produce the engines, others, including Smiths, work on the electronics (called avionics). All aircraft need electrical systems to control their flight, oversee the running of their engines, provide navigation systems and radar to help them reach their destination and be aware of other aircraft in the vicinity. All have a need for engineering technicians.

FOOD AND CHEMICALS

The food and chemicals industries are huge businesses and essential to our modern way of life. They include oil companies, pharmaceuticals firms, organisations that make soap, cosmetics, colourings and paints, food additives and preservatives, drinks and semi-solids like margarine. Biotechnology, the use of biological products in chemical reactions, is a fast growing part of this vast industry. It started with brewing and now includes a range of products from medicines and vaccines to diagnostic kits.

Many companies in the chemicals industry operate their plant 24 hours a day and seven days a week. Keeping it safe and fully operational provides many opportunities for engineering technicians. You could be working for an oil company exploring for oil, or in a chemical plant producing a big range of products. Proctor and Gamble and Unilever, for example, make detergents plus a whole range of household chemicals and foods. Shell and BP have refineries making not only petrol but plastics, tar for roads and the many biproducts of oil. They and numerous other firms in these industries all employ engineering technicians.

ELECTRICITY

Static electricity, which you get when you rub a balloon on your clothes and stick it to a wall, or the tingle you sometimes experience when you get out of a car, has been known for thousands of years. Yet the electric light bulb was only invented by Thomas Edison in 1879. Faraday worked out how to produce electricity by magnetic induction and Edison got the first electricity distribution system up and running. In Western civilisation we take electricity for granted these days but there is still a lot of work for electricians and mechanical technicians, producing and distributing that energy safely and making, installing and repairing electrical equipment. Employers include the electricity generating companies such as E.ON and British Energy, distributors like the National Grid and everyone who uses electricity including the construction industry who install it into new buildings.

TELECOMMUNICATIONS

Alexander Graham Bell invented the telephone, which developed into today's huge international business with telephone exchanges, telegraph poles and landlines, aerials and receivers, communications satellites and mobile phones. Isn't it just fantastic how telephones have changed? It doesn't seem so long ago that we were all using those red boxes in the street. Mobile phones can take a photo, video the scene, contact someone on the other side of the world and offer games to play. Several technologies are merging so you can now

DID YOU KNOW?

The Engineering Council is to introduce another qualification in 2009 — the ICT Tech — for engineering technicians working in information and communications technology.

find television, the internet, computer power and telecommunications all coming together.

Engineers have played a central role in these developments. We now have the third generation (3G) of mobile phones and inevitably there will be many more developments in the future.

The employers include equipment manufacturers such as Siemens and Nokia and telephone companies Vodafone and BT. There are also those who make satellites and service them while in orbit, internet service providers, broadcasting organisations, music businesses and many more.

Technicians are needed to develop and maintain telephone networks that rely on software and hardware. The hardware includes telephone exchanges, landlines (including sub-sea cables) and satellite communications via telephone masts and dishes attached to houses and offices.

ELECTRONICS

Electronics is the technology of the twentieth century. Charles Babbage was the first to invent a computer but it was a mechanical device. The first electronic computer did not arrive until the 1950s. This vast industry that made possible mobile phones, landing men on the moon, electronic control systems and much more is less than 60 years old. It depends on transistors, invented in 1947, and integrated circuits, which didn't arrive until 1959. They provided the technology to put a complicated electronic circuit onto a tiny silicon chip so you could carry it around in your mobile phone or laptop. Just think what an astonishing difference these have made to our way of life, especially our ability to communicate on a global scale. Placing computers in networks so they can communicate with one another is a much more recent development. Almost every device, from TV to security system, lift to motor car now includes an integrated circuit.

MEASUREMENT AND CONTROL

How do you measure a litre of petrol or a kilogram of sugar? How can you determine the pressure in a tyre or the temperature in a room? Most industrial processes are governed by sensors that help us to weigh and count things or measure temperatures, pressures or the flow of liquids. If, for example, you were running a chemical plant you would need to know how much of each chemical went in and what came out. To avoid explosions the temperature and pressure must be controlled and those working in the control room need instruments that tell them what is going on, just like the gauges in a car that tell you the speed, how much petrol and oil you have and the temperature of the engine.

In this sector you could either be employed as an engineering technician by the firms that produce control equipment, including sensors and instrumentation, or by those that use it such as manufacturing organisations or those operating in the security business. The equipment is used to monitor and control exactly what is going on.

MATERIALS

It's a material world and many engineering technicians are working with materials. There is a large variety and one for every possible use. They include metals, ceramics, plastics, glass, liquids, paper and textiles, and composites. Each has their own properties in terms of strength, conductivity of electricity or insulation, cracking, pliability and the range of temperatures in which they can safely be used.

If you decide to become an engineering technician working with materials you could be employed by a range of different employers. First are the producers of materials such as Pilkingtons (glass), Corus (steel), oil companies such as Shell and BP (plastics). Then there are those who take these materials and make them into something, like Ford or Phillips. This is a very large group that includes most of the aerospace industry, automotive industry, food manufacturers and makers of household and business equipment.

Extremely thin layers of materials, often only a few atoms thick, are used to produce the chips that go into electrical circuits and these have their own special properties. We are now quite used to seeing materials reinforced by carbon fibre, often seen in kitchen trays but initially introduced for the aerospace industry and space travel because they are light. When a new need arises engineers have to choose the best material for that purpose, so novel materials have been developed for such things as long-life light bulbs and sensors.

Now there is a much stronger emphasis on recycling materials that have been used. Engineering technicians are involved in all the processes that contribute to making materials and fashioning them into the shapes we need, including wire, plate, film and mouldings.

ENERGY AND WATER

In our modern society we all need what we call public utilities – gas, electricity and water. Last century we depended on coal to fire our power stations but now we use gas and oil and nuclear fuel. The 1980s brought a boom in North Sea oil and gas with engineers discovering it, installing platforms and devising the vast range of equipment needed to drill wells, extract oil and transport it by pipeline or tanker to the shore. Although it is now reducing, North Sea oil and gas is still an important industrial sector employing large numbers of engineering technicians. 'Roughnecks', as they are known, are engineering technicians who work on oil rigs to perform drilling operations, either prospecting for oil or to extract it from the wells. In the future we will rely more on nuclear power plus new technologies to get energy from biofuels, the sun, wind, waves and tides. Wherever there is energy to be generated, stored or distributed there are always engineering technicians.

We all need water and rely on companies in the water industry to gather and purify it before distributing it to our taps. The same firms also deal with waste water, including sewage. These are services essential to our survival which engineering technicians can be involved in.

DEFENCE AND CRIME

Our enemies and criminals are continually improving the technologies they use and to protect ourselves we must always stay one step ahead. Engineering for defence and warfare and crime detection is always at the cutting edge of technology. The government recently commissioned the building of two new aircraft carriers and there is a continual updating, production and maintenance of all defence equipment.

Firms like BAE Systems, recruiting 250 technicians a year, and Rolls-Royce, QinetiQ, Thales and Smiths employ engineering technicians to manufacture defence equipment supplying everything from submarines and aircraft through navigation and communication systems to weapons. Recently an unmanned surveillance aircraft was produced with image collection and data exploitation systems. The Army, Navy and RAF all need to keep equipment in a continual state of readiness and the Police and Home Office also seek the very best equipment in the fight against crime. This adds up to a lot of work for engineering technicians.

Everywhere we go these days we are seen on closed circuit TV. The speed of our cars is measured and number plates are read by roadside equipment.

These are just some of the industries in which you could work. There are more, including health (making implants such as hips and aids for the disabled) and education where the use of modern technology is vital as a learning tool.

Table 1 gives a list of where engineering technicians work in manufacturing, transport, energy, construction and communications.

Given this range of opportunities it is hardly surprising that here in the UK there is a dire shortage of engineering technicians. More people need to be trained to do these jobs in engineering if the UK is going to compete well with other countries around the world in engineering and high tech products. The Government is putting a great deal of support behind apprenticeships because they provide a mix of on-the-job experience and classroom training that will equip young

TABLE 1 SECTORS EMPLOYING ENGINEERING TECHNICIANS

Transport	Construction	Energy & IT
● Aviation	● Building Services	● Electricity Industry
● Marine Industry	Engineering	● Electrical and Electronic
● Motor Industry	● Mechanical	Services
● Rail Transport	Engineering services	● Information Technology and
	– Plumbing	Electronic Services
	● Heating, Ventilating,	● Communication Technologies
	Air Conditioning and	(Telecommunications)
	Refrigeration	● Gas Industry
		● Water Industry

people for the careers of the future. Apprenticeships provide a structured route into this career but some firms offer a less regulated approach to training which still offers the opportunity eventually to gain all the skills that are required.

According to the Institution of Mechanical Engineers there are more than one million people working as engineering technicians in the UK at the moment but it is not enough. More will be required in the years ahead because many now doing the jobs are reaching retirement age and a fall in the birth rate some years ago means that there will be fewer teenagers to consider this career in the next few years. The opportunities are there. You just need to go out and find them. This book shows you the way.

As an engineering technician it is not essential to join a professional engineering institution, but you can. There are now 31 professional bodies for engineering technicians covering every aspect of engineering in practice. Once you have trained and qualified they will offer you membership and the opportunity to put the letters EngTech after your name (Chapter 9, 'Further Information').

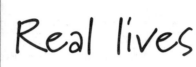

3 Real lives

In this chapter we talk to several engineering technicians about their experiences, what they do and how they got there.

ROBERT MANLEY

Robert Manley is a Precision Machinist employed at the Atomic Weapons Establishment, Aldermaston. 'I produce prototypes of tooling, jigs and positioning apparatus for the scientists here,' says Robert. 'My job involves using manual and CNC operated machines to fashion metal items to the required shapes. I work with a large range of metals including lead, aluminium, brass, steel and titanium and after two years in this role I feel like I have seen it all. Some of the materials worked have special safety requirements which make the job even more of a challenge. The work often involves programming the CNC machines for a specific one-off job. Colleagues often come with a scribbled drawing on paper and say "can you make this?" and it's a challenge I enjoy. Sometimes the parts I make also have to be assembled and can make quite impressive assemblies when complete.

'I left school at 16 because it didn't suit me and was not what I wanted. My hobby is making miniature petrol and steam engines and through this I was fortunate enough to already have some experience of using a lathe and other tools. I joined AWE as a Foundation Modern Apprentice and studied for a City & Guilds course at Basingstoke College. After the first year I moved onto the advanced Modern Apprenticeship Scheme, which added an extra year to the three-year foundation course. I studied for the BTEC ONC and the first year of the HNC at Newbury College. During the last two years of the programme I took three-month work placements in all of the different areas of the business. Since leaving the apprenticeship programme I have continued my studies and finished my HNC and my HND.

'One role I really enjoyed was the mentoring of students who come here for work experience. That has been very rewarding because three of the ten students I have worked with have taken up the opportunity to become apprentices themselves.

'I've now professionally qualified as an Engineering Technician with the Institution of Mechanical Engineers and will continue to progress my career this autumn by starting a degree course in mechanical engineering at Loughborough University.'

KATY DEACON

Katy Deacon started her career as an Avionic Trainee with British Airways. 'I began as an Aircraft Maintenance Apprentice,' says Katy. 'My basic training started at Perth Airport learning basic hand skills whilst studying for my HND in Aeronautical Engineering as well as taking my JAR66 industry licence exams. I also gained experience working on the maintenance and repair of aircraft systems on Boeing 737, 747 and Airbus A319 and A320 aircraft in the hangers at Heathrow, Cardiff and Manchester Airports. It was a four-year programme leading to my becoming an Aircraft Avionics Technician.

'I eventually decided to move out of the aircraft industry and broaden my experience,' says Katy. 'I was offered a job with Kirklees Council as an electrical Engineer's Assistant where I design and project manage rewires, security systems, emergency lighting systems and fire alarms within council-owned buildings including schools.

'I started as an Engineering Technician, then over the five years I've been with the council I've worked my way up from being an Engineer's Assistant through the ranks to become an Engineer. I've recently submitted my application to become a Chartered Engineer. At work, I'm now an Energy Engineer, responsible for the roll-out of Smart Metering across the council. I also support design teams when they are considering energy efficiency and renewable energy installations, particularly wind turbines and solar photovoltaic systems. I love it! Every day is different and my work is helping to reduce the carbon dioxide output of the whole district.'

MEGAN OLLIVERE

Megan Ollivere is an Engineering Technician working at Jaguar Cars test facility at Gaydon in the Midlands. Her job is to complete tests on any part of a vehicle that requires it. When a new component is designed, using computer-aided engineering, a prototype is made and this is then tested. Many of the tests are 'legislative', which means that it is a legal requirement that the car manufacturer carries them out.

'Any idea can be tested,' says Megan. 'They can be pre-production parts – those that have not yet been included in a vehicle – or parts that are in production but are perceived to have developed a problem. Often they are things like steering columns, brakes or brackets and we test them to destruction.

'I started my Jaguar career by completing an apprenticeship. You need five GCSEs including Maths, English and a science to get onto the scheme but I had also studied A levels in Maths, Physics and Geography. I was 18 when I began whereas most of the apprentices started straight from leaving school at 16.

'The first year of my apprenticeship was a full-time NVQ Level 2 course in Performing Engineering Operations at City College, Coventry. It included theoretical and practical studies on fitting and electrical maintenance.

'I spent the second year in my department. I started my ONC studies and attended college one day each week. It included studying information technology, maths and communication. We have several departments here including Design and Pilot Build but I chose to work in Safety Component Testing. There is lots of measurement, working out angles and analysing results.

'In the third year of my apprenticeship I started a Foundation Degree in Engineering, which I have almost finished. This was also completed by taking a day a week at college and making up the time by working extra hours in my department.

'I have gained experience by working on lots of different projects. For example, I investigated the feasibility of a new rig to test steering wheels and later designed a rig that tested if components complied with the legislation.

'It's been a really good experience. I've met Margaret Hodge when she was Minister of State for Industry and the Regions and taken projects into schools as a part of the Engineering Education Scheme to increase pupils' interest in engineering.'

A business of your own

Some engineering technicians start their own business. It's a major step to take and best done when you have gained a few years' experience but, as we see here, it is possible to be very successful.

BRIAN HOWE

Brian Howe trained as an electrician when he left school and was employed installing electrical fittings into new buildings. Some of the firms he was employed by fell on difficult times so he moved and in doing so gained a very broad experience. Most of his work was in the Islington area of London.

Eventually, when he was 27 years old, he decided to work for himself and looked around for contracts to complete electrical work. He wrote to Islington Council and much to his surprise they offered him a contract which included so much engineering work that he had to employ six other electricians to complete it. He also opened a shop in a small kiosk where he sold electrical items such as cables, switches, fuses, bulbs, light fittings, connections and other electrical goods.

Business grew to such an extent that Brian eventually gave up being an electrician himself and instead managed his company. Brian then moved to Barnet where his business has continued to thrive.

DANNY

Danny's first job was as a Technician in a car dealership. He did his apprenticeship working on all kinds of cars, their electrics and mechanical maintenance. He qualified as a member of the Institute for the Motor Industry and eventually decided to branch out on his own. Now he specialises in the maintenance of SAAB cars, has his own garage and two employees at TDL Car Care.

NEIL

Neil is an Electrical Engineer. Like Brian he learned his trade as an apprentice. Along the way he got interested in security systems and eventually set up his business, Insight Security, surveying premises, advising on the most appropriate security system and completing the installation.

4

What are the jobs?

AEROSPACE

Fascinated by aeroplanes? Would you like to fly? Not everyone working as a technician in aerospace actually flies as a part of their job but some do. All of them have an intimate knowledge of what goes into an aeroplane and how it works. The work includes the design, production, maintenance and repair of civil and defence aircraft, fixed wing and helicopters. It also includes work on satellites and the rockets required to get them into orbit. You could be making the parts, assembling them into airworthy products and maintaining them wherever in the world they might be.

Modellers convert design ideas into computer models and engineering drawings in preparation for the manufacture of parts. They use computer-assisted design software to give reality to the proposed designs and produce specifications for the parts that will be required.

Engine fitters assemble parts of an engine. There are mechanical and electrical components to be included in the construction, which they assemble in accordance with the technical drawings. It is very precise work and the measurement of each part is crucial to the final fit and operation of the entire engine.

Instrument technicians provide gauges to measure what is going on in the aircraft, such as how much fuel there is, and those that assist the pilot to control the flight. All of these instruments have to be calibrated, installed into place and connected to the parts of the plane they relate to.

Electrical fitters take the drawings of the electrical circuits within an aircraft and install the wiring and equipment. Then they test it. You may be working and crawling around in confined spaces from the wings to the fuselage. Everything from the lighting and air conditioning to the electrical fittings required to raise the undercarriage or change the configuration of the wings is included.

Machinists are those who make the parts. Each part of the engine has to be manufactured, often from a piece of metal. Machinists create the correct shapes by using turning, grinding and milling machines. They start with an engineering drawing and proceed to manufacture the part to the right shape and size and within exacting tolerances. They may simulate the forces acting on each part when the aircraft is in flight and test that it will withstand the conditions it is under.

When an engine is in service with an airline or an air force (not just the RAF) it must be maintained and repaired. This is a job for service engineers. There is a plan for regular maintenance but during a flight the air crew may discover a fault which needs to be rectified before the plane can take off safely again. Service engineers work anywhere around the world providing customers, those who own the aircraft, with an after-sales service. They are also involved if the customer needs their engines to be modified in some way, perhaps to reduce noise or increase fuel efficiency. Many of these engineers work on shifts that are organised so that their services are available 24 hours a day and seven days a week.

In aircraft it can be catastrophic if something goes seriously wrong so quality is very important. Quality engineers check that everything is in line with the specification and all the regulations that are in force.

Planning technicians work on planning and scheduling so that all the parts become available at the right time. It involves lots of detailed work including negotiating with suppliers and working out how the parts will get to the place for assembly.

AUTOMOTIVE
If you get a buzz out of cars or motorbikes you could be employed in the motor industry producing new vehicles, at a garage in the retail trade, maintaining a fleet of vehicles for a business, in motor racing or as someone who gives roadside assistance. You might even, eventually, work for yourself in car maintenance or bodywork (see Chapter 3, 'Real lives'). You can become a certified automotive engineer and progress to an advanced automotive engineer as your career progresses.

Fast-fit technicians work in a garage diagnosing faults for clients. They discuss problems with the owner of the vehicle then replace and repair faulty parts, installing new components. Modern motor vehicles are full of computers and electronics that help engineering technicians to diagnose what has gone wrong. Technicians specialise in many different areas such as mobile electronics and security, motorcycles and specific types of vehicles. Some focus their attention on body repairs to vehicles after they have had accidents or scrapes.

Roadside assistance technicians answer calls from drivers whose vehicles have let them down. To be successful in this role you need to be good with people and capable of dealing with them when they may be distressed. It is not just about being an engineer but having a good manner with customers and a focus on their needs. Technicians tend to do this when fully trained and qualified rather than during an apprenticeship but RAC takes on apprentices who start by being trained to replace windscreens. Their job is to attend vehicles in the street, discuss the problem with the driver and complete minor repairs that will get the customer home.

Working for a motor manufacturer the technology involved in producing vehicles is just fantastic. You could be dealing with robots, computer control systems that control the production processes and paint spraying. Modern vehicles contain lots of electronics that control the engine, fuel supply, heating and ventilating, navigation systems and hi-fi, so there is plenty for electronic technicians to get their teeth into. Brakes and suspension depend on pneumatic and hydraulic systems where again there are specialist technicians employed. Others are focused on the engines, making the parts or obtaining them from suppliers and assembling, testing and installing the entire engines into the vehicles. Bodywork is another key area, where sheet metal is pressed into panels for each section of the vehicle and plastic parts moulded before being ready for the assembly line. At Toyota you are trained to be multi-tasking so eventually you learn a wide range of technology.

The manufacturing plant is run by electrical systems, so the supply of electricity to each part of it must be safely installed and maintained.

FOOD AND CHEMICALS

You could be working in operations, optimising the process and making sure that they are both safe and environmentally responsible. The plant often works at high temperatures and pressures and needs effective, reliable technicians to make sure that nothing catastrophic can occur with terrible results, not only for the people working there but also those who live and work in close proximity to the plant.

The work includes troubleshooting problems that arise in the production process. The range of equipment may include chemical reactors, heat exchangers, pumps, compressors, turbines, valves, pressure vessels, tanks and pipework. As an engineering technician working in operations you will need to have a detailed understanding of how all the bits of equipment work and what to do when things go wrong.

You could be involved in maintaining every piece of equipment that goes up to make the complete process or have special responsibility for one section. Each one has a schedule of planned maintenance, but problems in the plant may bring forward some activities and delay others. When demand for the product is high it may be difficult to close down a process entirely to complete the maintenance.

Sometimes this is done at weekends and during nights when the plant is not operating but those processes that run continuously, such as producing petrol in the oil industry, always have detailed plans for when big maintenance operations or the introduction of new equipment will occur. Conditions in the plant must be optimised to produce the highest quality products in the most efficient way.

You could be taking samples of the chemicals at many different stages in the process on a regular basis and analysing them in the laboratory to check that they are as they should be. When the time comes for equipment to be maintained or repaired your first step would often be to isolate it from the rest of the process, cool it down, empty the contents and make it ready for inspection.

Helping chemical engineers to design, assemble and install new pieces of processing equipment is another role. You will be following safety guidelines to be sure that everything is safe. You could also be installing sensors and gauges and calibrating them to provide the measurements you need to monitor what is going on in the plant and run it efficiently. Alternatively you might be running the process, making adjustments when required or if things go wrong.

MATERIALS

In metals you could be operating processes that get the metal out of its ore. Alternatively you might be moulding it into ingots by preparing and using sand moulds or fettling (smoothing out imperfections in the items that come out of the moulds). If you are involved with making wire the metal will be forced through a dye (a hole the diameter you want the wire to be) under immense pressure and at a high temperature. Sheet metal is produced by rolling it between rollers just as you do with pastry and a rolling pin but using much more force. As an engineering technician you might be responsible for supervising any of these processes.

Working with plastics you might be operating an injection moulding machine that creates articles that are required or processing the material into thread, sheet or film.

Engineering technicians also investigate what has happened when materials fail through cracking or fatigue. They use microscopes and testing techniques to discover the cause of any particular failure. They also consider how the materials they use in their products could be improved to make better articles for their customers.

When making electronic materials and circuits they can be depositing very thin layers of materials onto 'chips' in vacuum (often around flat pieces of silicon). Later they test these circuits to make sure that they work correctly.

When making composite materials, technicians can be responsible for mixing the components and using moulds to set them into a shape. Satellites sometime include papier-mâché, which technicians apply in layers with glue.

It's a fascinating area. Just think of all the different types of material you use in a day and you will realise what an immense amount of the effort engineering technicians put into providing it all.

MEASUREMENT AND CONTROL

Control engineering technicians design, produce and install sensors and instrumentation required to control and monitor situations. This usually includes installing a control panel that allows the operator to know what is going on. A good understanding of electricity and electronics is essential as gauges have to be calibrated so that they indicate the right measurement. Technicians maintain and repair both sensors and instrumentation when they break down in service.

You can be making control equipment from scratch or putting it together from parts supplied by others. Alternatively you might work for an organisation that uses it in the automation of its production, including the counting, weighing, testing and wrapping of manufactured goods. Electronically controlled robots are often used to perform processes, carry parts around a plant or spray paint and every move they make is carefully controlled.

Things you might work on include lifts, heating and ventilating, and systems that control temperature and sometimes the humidity. Another role is the installation and maintenance of closed circuit television and security systems, often including sensors that detect movement or body heat.

TELECOMMUNICATIONS

Working in telecommunications you could train to install and repair telephones in people's homes. Not only do you need good technical skills but also the tact and diplomacy to deal with customers who may not always be in the best frame of mind. You might help to maintain telecommunication services by seeking out faults in the network such as the wiring and circuits in the communication boxes you see dotted around many streets, the antenna used to receive signals and transmission equipment. It can include climbing up telephone poles to make repairs. Naturally, for this kind of work it is essential to be able to drive a van, so BT insists that you get a full driving licence within a year of joining.

Technicians who work on these problems are situated all over the country and work out of local bases, so it may not be necessary to move away from home.

BT maintains its own fleet of vehicles, so one of the jobs it recruits into is vehicle maintenance. Technicians working in this area are employed to keep their vans and cars continually in service. The equipment includes the generators and racks within the vehicles that are required to house all the tools maintenance technicians require.

When a company installs a new network for all its computers and telephones this can be quite a task. Those technicians responsible are called 'narrow band and copper planners'. Imagine routing cable around a building so that telephones and computers can be conveniently located. Using 'bluetooth' wireless technology each piece of equipment can communicate with the others without the need for wires.

Another important role is that of keeping the network up and running, locating faults and passing the information on to the maintenance team. This is the responsibility of those employed in network planning.

Alternatively you could be working for a manufacturer making the pieces that go to producing equipment such as mobile phones, cables, aerials and other associated equipment.

MECHANICAL ENGINEERING
As a mechanical engineering technician you could be making the tiniest screw or the largest turbine (Robert Manley in Chapter 3). How this is done depends, of

course, on the materials that are being used. Metals can be turned on a lathe, milled, ground, drilled, extruded at high temperature, bent, hammered or in some other way coaxed into the required shape. Plastics may be moulded but the engineers will first have to manufacture the moulds.

Complicated things, like a bicycle or a hairdryer, need several parts to be designed and fashioned so each one fits in precisely with all the others. It requires careful consideration of the function each part will play in the whole product, what it will be made of, who will produce it and how it will be assembled.

Naturally mechanical technicians often have to work with other engineers. A dishwasher, a mobile phone or a computer will also have electrical and electronic parts and whatever the mechanical engineer makes must take account of this. So it is essential to work in teams with others.

A chemical plant or oil installation needs piping and vessels to be made. Whatever the product it will be necessary to discuss with others the exact requirements, interpret the engineering drawings and make the piece of equipment.

Laying and maintaining railway track and rolling stock is another prominent area. You could also be employed in a power station and working on power lines or making medical equipment such as wheelchairs, hip joints and articles to help the disabled.

So you could be shaping and manufacturing parts in the machine shop and interpreting drawings to make a specific part or several parts that will eventually fit together to make something else. It is an exacting role requiring precise measurement. Eventually all the parts will be assembled to make the complete article – another job for the engineering technician.

The care and maintenance of each piece of equipment may be your responsibility and eventually you could be supervising a workshop, part of a production line or the design of parts in a drawing office.

ENERGY

As an engineering technician you could be employed by an oil company to explore for oil using seismic equipment or drill for oil, often in out-of-the-way places. You could be making and constructing equipment such as oil platforms or pumps and pipelines to get the oil to its destination. Alternatively you might be installing sensors and instrumentation that allow the flow of oil from the wellhead to be controlled by radio from a distance.

Working with an electricity generator you could be monitoring the turbines and maintaining and repairing equipment. Another role is installing instrumentation to monitor and adjust the performance of generators and to network the electrical power into the national grid. Mechanical fitters undertake planned overhauls of turbines, boilers and other equipment.

Working for a manufacturer you could be making parts of specific pieces of equipment including cables for electricity conduction, instrumentation to run the plant and the entire

range of bits and pieces that go into a turbine generator.
Like an aero engine it's a dynamic piece of machinery with
parts whizzing round at high speeds. You might also be
providing an after-sales service to your customers for when
something goes wrong.

Technicians work on the installation and commissioning of
pylons and overhead lines and most often their maintenance
and repair. You will need a head for heights since you could
be travelling along an electricity line on a cradle high above
the ground or up a pylon. Safety is a big factor. A second
role is dealing with problems that occur in electricity sub-
stations located near to people's homes.

You can, of course, train to be an electrician who installs,
checks and tests electricity in homes, offices, public
buildings and streets for lighting, heat and to run the
numerous pieces of equipment that modern premises
have. Manufacturers, of whatever variety, need electricians
to maintain electricity supply to their production equipment.
In some case, such as where extremely high temperatures
must be obtained in the heating of blast furnaces, the
electricity supply is a crucial element of the process.

DEFENCE

Working in defence you could be responsible for electronic
communication and information systems, installing equipment
where it is required or as an operator of telecommunications
systems. Your job could involve understanding, maintaining
and repairing electronic circuitry or being responsible for the
supply of technical equipment to groups deployed abroad
and sometimes in the front line of battle.

Another role is the servicing and inspection of the vast range of electrical and mechanical equipment the forces use. In warfare it is essential that all the equipment is reliably maintained and operates well, even in conditions where the climate or the terrain make their operation difficult. Wherever you are and whatever the climate, equipment must be speedily repaired when required. This includes everything from motor vehicles and battle tanks through to helicopters.

Some engineering technicians are involved in the engineering that takes place during a combat. Their work ranges from providing fortifications for the troops through to putting bridges in place to get people and equipment across rivers and constructing or demolishing roads. They are also the experts who have the job of neutralising explosive devices.

There are two types of aircraft technician. Avionics technicians maintain and repair the electronic equipment in the aircraft that is essential to its operation including navigation, engine controls and communication systems. Mechanical aircraft technicians deal with almost everything else on board. This includes most things from the airframe, engines and propulsion systems down to tiny mechanical components.

Electrical technicians are responsible for all electrical equipment such as power units, portable generators and electrical installations. Mechanical technicians deal with such things as the maintenance and repair of vehicles, hydraulic lifts, fuel tankers, fire engines, cranes and cars.

Workshop technicians, as their name implies, work in the workshop where they could be using milling machines, lathes, grinding equipment and welding tools to repair or make new parts that the aircraft requires.

Weapons technicians have responsibility for all the weapon systems on fighter and bomber aircraft. They load each aeroplane with more weaponry after a sortie so that it is ready to go out again and they make sure that the weapon release systems all work.

Tools of the trade

What kind of person do you need to be if you want to make a successful career as an engineering technician? What skills will you require?

First and foremost you will be doing a job that is practical. You will need some practical skills before you start and be keen to develop these to a greater degree as you progress. You must enjoy using your hands to make or mend things, to improve situations. Feeling at home working with machines and equipment and not being daunted by them is important. If you enjoy clasping a piece of machinery, examining it with all of your senses and in your mind's eye seeing how it will work, then you're halfway there. Engineering is a precise discipline where things are often measured to thousandths of an inch. Items made must fit exactly and look right in their place. It helps if you are the kind of person who likes this attention to detail.

Most engineering technicians work in an engineering environment. It may be a workshop, a factory, a drawing office. These are often noisy places where there is lots of activity and it is essential to feel comfortable working in that kind of situation. Some travel to other places to provide their services and these must enjoy the independence that it brings but also the responsibility to turn up and complete the job.

In your work as an engineering technician you have to be methodical. Know where your tools are and how to take care that they are kept in good order to be used the next time. If you borrow equipment from another technician they will expect it back and in good condition for them to use.

It is essential to understand the tasks you are set and work out the sequence of steps you will need to take in order to achieve your goal. Problem solving skills are important and often, especially in a maintenance or repair situation, they start with a diagnosis of what exactly is wrong.

DID YOU KNOW?

The Health and Safety Executive monitors workplaces to ensure that employers look after the safety of their staff and abide by legal safety requirements.

Safety is the top priority. In engineering you cannot simply rush about or do things that are reckless. There are set procedures to be followed and rules to be kept, such as using safety equipment and guards on machines. This is something you must be prepared to do in a self-disciplined way if you want to succeed.

In some areas of engineering, especially electrical work, colour blindness can create difficulties. A good awareness of colour is at least helpful and sometimes essential.

Communication is also very important. You will be communicating technical ideas by drawings, in writing and speaking to your colleagues and also people outside your normal working environment. First you will need to have the ability to communicate with colleagues who understand the technology you are working with and that includes having knowledge of all the relevant words, the jargon related to it. Second you must be able to communicate well with technologists from outside the firm, perhaps people who are selling you equipment. Third you have also to discuss proposals with employees in other departments, such as marketing, who cannot be expected to understand the fine detail or the engineering jargon.

Drawings are often the best way to communicate concepts in engineering and in many areas of work you will be given an engineering drawing and asked to make or repair something based upon what it tells you. It is helpful if you can draw. You don't need to be an artist but a good understanding of geometry is a major advantage. There will also be some calculations, so you should have a facility with numbers rather than run a mile when they come up.

Often of most significance is the ability to communicate with customers. If you are in a role where you provide a service to someone, such as in a garage or as an installer of equipment, then you have to display an entirely different range of skills. When a customer is distressed or annoyed you will need some charm and especially the ability to be tactful and diplomatic. Those who find it easy to deal with people in stressful situations will enjoy this role but there is always a need to give customers realistic expectations of how and when they will have their needs met.

Having read this you might think that super human skills are required to be an engineering technician. But you don't have to have all these skills when you start out on this career. Many of them come as you develop, experience the situations at first hand and learn how to cope with them. Decide the course of action for your career, work hard and the tools of your trade will come along in due course.

FAQs

Why should I want to be an Engineering Technician?
Because, if you are a practical, common sense kind of person who enjoys solving technical problems you will do things in engineering you will be proud of. Then you can say 'I did that!' As an engineering technician you can see the results of what you have achieved whether it is a piece of equipment you made or one you got to work. If you enjoy working with people you can choose technical jobs that give a customer service and give other people satisfaction as well as yourself.

Qualifying as an engineering technician is not a dead end. It can lead to more qualifications and management roles or self-employment.

Where can I work?
There are jobs for engineering technicians just about everywhere. We saw in Chapters 2 and 4 a broad range of industries you might work in.

Could I work abroad?
Yes. Engineering technicians develop a set of skills that allows them to get work not just in the UK but also overseas. As an engineering technician the world really is your oyster.

Do I have to do an apprenticeship?
No. It is not essential to complete an apprenticeship, though this is the easiest route to professional qualification. To become a fully qualified engineering technician you will need to reach a Level 3 academic qualification and be able to demonstrate all the skills required by your professional body. However, by no means all Engineering Technicians are members of a professional body.

I don't want to do an apprenticeship. What are my options?
Some people prefer to gain further qualifications before taking up a job and it is possible to become an engineering technician this way. You would need to study engineering-related qualifications at college and then take up a trainee job with an engineering firm to put the theory into practice. This route can also lead to formal qualification and membership of a professional body if you can demonstrate you have all the skills and knowledge required to do the job.

What qualifications would I need?
You would probably study for a BTEC National Certificate in Engineering that interests you. City & Guilds also offer a number of engineering qualifications that would be relevant. Entry requirements for these courses are usually five GCSEs grades A–C but you can start by taking a BTEC Introductory Certificate without any previous qualifications (Chapter 7).

APPRENTICESHIPS

What are the benefits of an apprenticeship?
An apprenticeship gives you both the training and the experience you need to become a professional Engineering

Technician and also provides a salary while you study. It will lead to qualifications that potential employers recognise. It could increase your employability and, if all goes well, lead to a job offer at the end.

I want to do an apprenticeship. When should I apply?
Most firms recruit apprentices in the spring during the period from December to the end of May. Check on firms' websites for details or ask at your local Connexions office.

What are the minimum requirements?
GCSEs in Maths, Science and English at grade C and above are almost always required for an apprenticeship but some firms demand higher academic qualifications of up to five GCSEs.

When will I start my apprenticeship?
Most apprenticeship schemes start in September but once qualified you can find opportunities all year round.

Is there much competition for places?
Yes, there can be. Some firms receive as many as 20 applications for every place, but the less-well-known organisations get fewer. You will have to spend time completing your application well and prepare for interview by getting to know as much as you can about the firm and their apprenticeship programme. You can get help with this from Connexions.

How long does an apprenticeship last?
Typically between three and four years.

How much will I be paid as an apprentice?

The minimum pay an apprentice can receive is £80 per week (2008) but many employers pay very much more than this, typically £9,000 p.a. According to a recent survey by SEMTA, apprentices working in electrical/electronic industries earn the most, followed by those in engineering manufacture. Updating the figures for inflation, the average weekly apprentice wage in the industries below is now (Spring 2008) around:

- Electronics/Electrical   £197
- Engineering Manufacture   £179
- Construction   £152
- Motor   £146

What would I be studying?

Apprentices begin their studies with a course where they learn the basics – how to work safely and efficiently, how to use the tools of their trade and key skills. Once qualified you still need to attend regular training courses to keep abreast of changes in technology.

What qualifications will I study for?

By the end of your apprenticeship you will gain a National Vocational Qualification (NVQ) Level 3 in your chosen area of engineering. This signals to employers that you can do everything that is expected of you as an engineering technician. During your training you will qualify with an NVQ Level 2 and complete a BTEC National Certificate (NC) or City & Guilds qualification.

Will I study full-time or part-time?

Some employers send you to college or another training provider on full-time courses for the first year. Others send you to college for a few days each week.

Where will I study?
Courses of study for trainee engineering technicians are offered at local colleges of further education. You can, if you wish, simply enrol and complete a course. Many trainees are sent by their firms to specialist training organisations, which the employers pay for, and a few companies run their own training schools.

If I go away to study will I get help in seeking accommodation?
Yes. When firms send you away from home to study they also provide help with accommodation.

What will I do when I'm at work?
That depends very much on the area of engineering you decide to join. You will be learning and training on the job, sometimes by watching others but also by completing tasks that are within your capability but will increase your competence in a range of technical activities.

Do I have to buy my own tools?
No. It is usual for the employer to buy these and any special clothing that you might need to wear at work such as safety shoes and goggles.

How many days' leave will I get in a year?
When you are employed as an apprentice you are also entitled to at least 20 days' holiday a year plus bank holidays. As an experienced engineer you may get longer after a certain duration of service.

AT WORK

What are the normal working hours?
Normal working hours for engineering technicians are around 37.5 hours a week. When you work can vary

a great deal from one situation to another. Many work a normal nine-to-five day, but if you are repairing aircraft or maintaining a chemical plant you could well be working seven- or eight-hour shifts at any time of the day or night.

Once I'm qualified, what will I earn?

Salaries for engineering technicians vary greatly between sectors and parts of the country but you could expect to start on anything between £18,000 and £25,000 per year depending on your skills and experience. This can rise quite quickly as you gain experience. According to an Engineering Council survey in 2007, average earnings for engineering technicians were reportedly £37,599 not including bonuses or overtime.

Will I be expected to work overtime?

Yes, sometimes it will be necessary. Over 70% of engineering technicians recently surveyed said that they worked overtime.

Will I be paid extra if I work overtime?

Usually yes. Most employers do offer payment for overtime that is worked.

What are the job prospects?

The job prospects are extremely good. There is currently a severe shortage of engineering technicians. In a recent survey the Engineering Council found that fewer than 2% of engineering technicians were unemployed.

What are the opportunities for career development?
Qualified engineering technicians can, if they wish, train
and study to become Chartered Engineers. This involves
taking a degree and gaining further experience. Katy Deacon
in Chapter 3 has done this and Robert Manley is preparing
to do so.

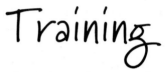

Training

There are many routes to becoming an engineering technician. Some start with Young Apprenticeships, others complete their GCSEs before starting their technical training. Some leave school without the qualifications they need and decide at a later stage to take Technical Certificates, BTEC or City & Guilds qualifications instead of GCSEs. A few finish their A levels and then choose to train as an engineering technician.

QUALIFICATIONS

To start on the way to becoming an engineering technician you will need a minimum of three GCSEs at grades C and above in Maths, Science and English. You could study to a higher level if you wish and still become one.

The biggest change coming up is the introduction of diplomas for 14–19 year olds. From September 2008 some schools will be offering Foundation Diplomas in the three subjects – engineering, information technology, and construction and the built environment. Each Foundation Diploma is equivalent to three GCSEs at grades D to G but you will need more than this to start a career as an engineering technician. The Higher Diploma is equivalent to seven GCSEs grades A* to C and this qualification will be acceptable by most of the recruiters. If you wish you can continue and complete the advanced diploma, which is equivalent to three and a half A levels. This is way above the normal academic requirement for entry into a career as an engineering technician but may stand you in good stead to progress your career later on.

The Engineering Diploma does not train you to be an engineer but it does give you the opportunity to explore and develop the skills you will need if you decide to make your career as an engineering technician. These studies offer an insight into engineering principles, design, materials, electronic systems, maintenance and manufacturing and will combine classroom teaching with real hands-on experience. At the outset diplomas will not be available everywhere and GCSEs will continue to be available and accepted by employers.

Young Apprenticeships
For those who want to start early, get more real work experience sooner and not spend all their time in school, the Young Apprenticeship Programme is attractive. Young apprenticeships are for 14–16 year olds who prefer practical and applied subjects to theoretical classroom studies. Started in 2004 with 1,000 students, in 2008 the scheme had grown to include 9,000 people. It includes Young Apprenticeships in Engineering, the Motor Industry and Construction.

Young apprentices continue to study maths, science, English and Information and Communications Technology (ICT) at school but spend 50 days over the two years of the programme with an employer gaining valuable work experience. They also attend college for training in their chosen field. Your school, local Connexions or learning and skills council will have full details of the programme, which can also be found on the www.apprenticeships.org website.

Other routes

If you have left school and do not have the necessary qualifications another route is to study the BTEC First Certificate in Engineering. It can also be gained in Vehicle Technology and Information and Communications Technology (ICT). These are all equivalent to the three GCSEs you need to begin an engineering technician career. If you first need to build up your confidence to get to this level, an Introductory Certificate in Engineering (BTEC) will get you there.

If you have reached your mid-twenties and decide you now want to train as an engineering technician or even change career into this area of work, don't despair. You can. There is no age limit to doing an apprenticeship and you may find you qualify more quickly than your younger contemporaries as you will bring additional skills and experience to the job that they won't have. Of course, the completion of an apprenticeship is not essential when training to become an Engineering Technician and you may be able to take up a trainee role at an engineering firm and follow a more unstructured training programme that will ensure you develop all the skills you will require.

THE NEXT STEP

Having completed the academic requirements the next step is to apply for an apprenticeship or find an employer who offers on-the-job training. More than 250,000 people in England are currently completing apprenticeships and the Government is committed to doubling this figure over the next few years. What an opportunity! Employers each set their minimum qualifications when selecting candidates, which may be higher than those mentioned above.

As we have seen in Chapters 2 to 4, you can work as an engineering technician in many different areas of engineering so there is lots of choice. There are 180 different apprenticeships available in 80 industries. Not all of these are for engineers but you can see from these figures that there is such a vast range that it is likely that one will suit you. If an apprenticeship does not appeal to you, you can still join a company and train for the job without going through an apprenticeship programme. The key areas are electrical and electronics, mechanics, aeronautics, chemical, construction and the environment. If your passion is cars or aeroplanes you could be working with them. If it is electricity, gas or oil there are jobs in these too. Whatever your interests, there are opportunities to match.

If you become an apprentice you commit yourself to between three and four years of intensive training. Some of Britain's largest firms, such as Network Rail, have their own training facilities and send trainees there for their first year. With some firms this can mean moving away from home. Most have a partnership with a training provider, which are sometimes a local college of further education and often a private training organisation. You can get details of apprenticeship training organisations from your local Connexions and the Learning and Skills Council.

What you will learn is very broad-ranging, including not only basic engineering and practical skills but also how to work safely and efficiently in what you will be doing and communicate effectively with other technical staff.

> **DID YOU KNOW?**
>
> The Learning and Skills Council is proposing a National Skills Academy to 'change the face of skills training'.

Engineering environments can be dangerous if not treated with respect, so the first thing you learn is not only to be safe yourself but to look out for the safety of other people too.

There are many different modes of training. In some organisations it is clearly laid down and rigidly applied and in other firms a more flexible approach is taken. While some aspiring engineering technicians complete their initial studies on a full-time basis, known as 'block release', others attend college for a day or more each week, a scheme called 'day release'. Some argue that it is best to complete the studies and then apply them in practice while others think it best to learn some things and then quickly apply what you have learnt in the work place. During college holidays apprentices work full time at their employer's premises.

THE WAY IN

Training includes both work-based learning and training. One way in is to approach employers directly. Most of the large employers have websites that include a careers section. This usually holds details of their vacancies for trainees and apprenticeship programmes. Some provide profiles of people who are currently apprentices, which give you an excellent flavour of what it is like. They also provide full details of their programme, how it operates, what you will be studying, where you will be and what qualifications you will achieve.

Another approach is to get in touch with your local Connexions or learning and skills council who will give you information of organisations that provide training and apprenticeships. If you know already which area of engineering you would like to work in, each area has a Sector Skills Council and you can discover much more information from their websites (see Chapter 9, 'Further information'). Following this route you apply for a place on a training course and take advantage of the fact that the training organisations work closely with a number of employers to provide them with apprentices. They have close contact with the employers for which they provide training and can put you forward for selection.

Applications for apprenticeships are usually made in the period between December and May and are followed by a selection procedure that always involves an interview and may also include other exercises and a tour of the premises of the organisation you intend to join. Apprenticeships normally begin in the early autumn.

If you have left school and don't have the necessary qualifications another route is to study the BTEC First Certificate in Engineering. It can also be gained in Vehicle Technology and Information and Communications Technology (ICT). These are all equivalent to the three GCSEs you need to begin an engineering technician career. If you first need to build up your confidence to get to this level an Introductory Certificate in Engineering will get you there.

DID YOU KNOW?

Government is putting more finance into apprenticeships for the over-25s.

WHAT YOU LEARN

In the engineering sector an apprenticeship can last up to five years, though it is more usual for it to take between three-and-a-half and four years. To complete it successfully you have to be committed to training, study and work experience. All apprenticeships lead to a National Vocational Qualification at Level 3 plus a National Certificate. They are designed to develop your technical skills in understanding, using and applying the relevant technology that you will need in your chosen sector of work. They also enhance your key transferable skills in such areas as the application of numbers, teamwork, problem solving and communication.

Along the way you will get technical certificates such as BTEC or City & Guilds qualifications that relate to the area of technology in which you work.

City & Guilds Technical certificates you can choose include:

- Process Technology
- Vehicle Fitting
- Electrical and Electronic Servicing
- Motor Vehicle Technician
- Heating and Ventilating
- Refrigeration and Air conditioning
- Car Body Repair

Corus, the steelmaker, for example, has its apprentices based full-time at college during their first year. There they complete an NVQ Level 2 in Performing Engineering Operations, the first year of a National Certificate, six modules of key skills, a City & Guilds course in iron and steel making and an outdoor development course. While the initial stages of training cover subjects that are common to all engineering technicians, the later years provide the opportunity to specialise in the specific area of engineering you want to eventually be qualified in.

A TYPICAL APPRENTICESHIP TRAINING PROGRAMME

Year 1

- Full-time study at a training organisation or college

- Study Performing Engineering Operations* to NVQ Level 2 including:

- Safety and Efficient Working Practices

- Learn how to use the tools and machines of your trade – e.g. lathes, milling machines, grinding, welding, basic electrical wiring and testing circuits (different skills depending on the area of engineering you are in)

- Learn Key Skills – Application of number
  Communication
  Working with others
  Problem solving
  Information technology
  How to improve your own
    learning skills and performance

- National Certificate in a relevant subject.

Year 2

- On-the-job training

- Placements in departments where you will learn relevant skills, techniques, operations etc

- Projects

- Attend College some days each week or for a block of time

- Complete National Certificate
- Start NVQ Level 3.

Years 3/4
- Attend college for some days each week or a block of time
- Some firms provide 'Outward Bound' type training
- Complete NVQ Level 3
- Some firms offer a personal development programme covering subjects such as working with customers, teamwork, making presentations, managing your time
- On-the-job training in several placements possibly in different departments
- If you achieve excellent results you may be offered the chance to study for a Higher National Diploma or a Foundation Degree.

*Those in a manufacturing situation may study Performing Manufacturing Operations instead of Performing Engineering Operations

Performing Engineering Operations
Most apprentices in electrical, electronic, mechanical and production engineering begin by studying the NVQ in Performing Engineering Operations. It is studied at Levels 2 and 3. Level 2 includes three mandatory sections and many options from which you can choose two that relate to what you want to do eventually.

Mandatory subjects include health and safety, issues that are absolutely essential. Engineering environments can be dangerous places if people do not take care in everything that they do to protect themselves and the people they work with. 'Working safely' is the first module and is followed by 'Working efficiently and effectively'. Learning to do things in an orderly manner saves time and is a key to the profitability of each operation. The third mandatory module is 'Communicating technical information'. As an engineer you have to read and understand technical drawings, as well as communicate ideas to others in your own drawings. You also have to understand the language of your subject and use words that your fellow technicians use to describe equipment, techniques and processes.

Next there are a series of 32 units from which you can choose just two. If you are intending to progress into mechanical engineering you might choose making components; assembling components; using lathes, milling and grinding machines; cutting and shaping sheet metal. As an electrical technician your choice could be wiring electrical equipment; assembling and wiring electrical panels; carrying out routine servicing of electrical equipment or assembling electronic circuits.

Optional units in NVQ Level 2 include:

- Making components using hand tools
- Cutting and shaping sheet metal
- Using lathes and turning operations
- Assembling mechanical components
- Using welding equipment
- Wiring electrical equipment and circuits

- Assembling and wiring electrical panels
- Routine servicing of electrical equipment
- Making sand moulds and cores for casting
- Heat treating engineering materials
- Hand forging
- Using milling machines
- Carrying out pipe fitting activities
- Using grinding machines
- Pipe fitting
- Cutting sheet metal
- Brazing and soldering
- Assembling electronic circuits
- Making composite mouldings
- Manually casting components
- Fettling cast components
- Applying surface treatments
- Applying surface coatings

Optional units in NVQ Level 3 include:
- Producing mechanical engineering drawings using computer assisted design (CAD)
- Producing electrical and electronic engineering drawings using CAD
- Making components using hand fitting techniques
- Producing mechanical assemblies
- Forming and assembling pipework
- Preparing and using milling machines
- Preparing and using grinding machines
- Maintaining mechanical devices and equipment
- Preparing and using CNC turning machines
- Assembling and testing fluid power equipment
- Cutting and shaping materials using thermal cutting equipment

- Preparing and using arc welding equipment
- Preparing and using flame brazing and bronze welding equipment
- Producing and preparing sand moulds and cores for casting
- Wiring and testing electrical equipment and circuits
- Assembling, wiring and testing electrical panels
- Maintaining electrical equipment
- Maintaining and testing process instrumentation and control devices
- Producing component assemblies
- Fettling, finishing and checking cast components
- Stripping and rebuilding sports car engines
- Diagnosis and rectifying faults in motorsport vehicle systems.

There are many options concerned with welding, brazing and soldering. Others focus on forming materials into shape such as composite moulding; casting metals, forging engineering materials and applying surface coatings.

At Level 3 of the NVQ the same mandatory units are repeated but at a more advanced level. Additionally there are three units to choose from no less than 61 options. Some of these are concerned with using shaping machines such as computer numerically controlled (CNC) milling, grinding, turning. Others are involved in metal joining techniques. There is a unit on producing engineering drawings using computer assisted design systems. In short you can choose whatever studies you wish that relate to your chosen job function when you are qualified.

The National Certificate

After completing the NVQ, and sometimes before, many recruits commence studies for a BTEC National Certificate. These take two years and can be studied in a range of subjects including:

● Communications Technology
● Aerospace Engineering
● Electrical/Electronic Engineering
● Manufacturing Engineering
● Mechanical Engineering
● Operations and Maintenance Engineering
● Vehicle Technology
● Vehicle Motorsports.

DID YOU KNOW?

Continuing professional development, once you are fully trained, includes courses on manufacturers' products, private reading and study, attending courses and in-house conferences, assisting others and on-the-job learning.

These are the elements of an apprenticeship leading to professional qualification as an engineering technician. You can, with some employers, arrange to complete these without having a formal apprenticeship. Learning does not stop here, however. You will certainly receive continuing professional development training once your apprenticeship is complete and you may go on to study higher qualifications including a Foundation degree, an HND or a degree.

The last word

We have mentioned several advantages of being an engineering technician but there are more. The engineering profession has a system it calls 'Ladders and Bridges', which means that your career can progress as far as your talent will take you if you are prepared to study more and gain additional skills and experience.

Once you have become an engineering technician you can study a Higher National Diploma or Foundation Degree that relates to your work. Employers often sponsor their employees through these studies so finance is not usually an issue. Success in these can get you onto the second year of an honours degree course and completion of this plus the ability to demonstrate a specified level of skills can lead to the professional status of Incorporated Engineer.

Further study up to the level of a Master's degree and the demonstration of additional competence can help you achieve the highest professional engineering qualification of Chartered Engineer.

Another advantage of being an engineering technician is that you may be able to start your own business. Many do, as we saw in Chapter 3, 'Real lives'.

There are countless opportunities in engineering to be employed, self-employed or to gain experience and eventually run a business of your own.

Previous chapters have delved deep into what an engineering technician does, how you become one, the training and expertise, the diversity of opportunities. Having read this book, consider seriously whether it is something you could do and something you would want to be. The best careers are those where people pay us for doing the things we enjoy. Answer the questions in the quiz opposite as honestly as you can and it might help you to decide.

WOULD YOU MAKE A GOOD ENGINEERING TECHNICIAN?

TRY OUR QUIZ

✔ TICK YES OR NO

DO YOU WANT TO EARN A SALARY WHILE YOU LEARN?
☐ YES
☐ NO

WILL YOU GET GCSE PASSES GRADE C OR ABOVE IN MATHS, SCIENCE AND ENGLISH?
☐ YES
☐ NO

DO YOU ENJOY DOING PRACTICAL THINGS AT SCHOOL OR COLLEGE?
☐ YES
☐ NO

DO YOU ENJOY MAKING THINGS?
☐ YES
☐ NO

DO YOU LIKE TAKING THINGS APART AND PUTTING THEM TOGETHER AGAIN?
☐ YES
☐ NO

HAVE YOU EVER MADE MODELS?
☐ YES
☐ NO

DO YOU PREFER TO SEE AND TOUCH WHAT YOU HAVE DONE RATHER THAN HAVE IT HIDDEN, LIKE ACCOUNTS OR COMPUTER SOFTWARE?
☐ YES
☐ NO

WHEN SOMETHING NEEDS MENDING DO YOU LIKE TO TRY TO REPAIR IT?
☐ YES
☐ NO

IS IT BETTER TO GET THINGS DONE RATHER THAN PORE OVER THEORIES?
☐ YES
☐ NO

DO YOU LIKE DOING THINGS IN A CAREFUL, METHODICAL WAY, STEP BY STEP?
☐ YES
☐ NO

IS FIGURING OUT HOW THINGS WORK IN PRACTICE BETTER THAN READING ABOUT IT?
☐ YES
☐ NO

WHEN THINGS GO WRONG WITH SOMETHING TECHNICAL CAN YOU COMMUNICATE THE SITUATION TO PEOPLE WHO DON'T UNDERSTAND TECHNICAL THINGS?
☐ YES
☐ NO

ARE YOU KEEN TO LEARN BOTH AT WORK AND AT COLLEGE?
☐ YES
☐ NO

Answer 'YES' to most of these questions and this is a career you should consider. Answer 'NO' and perhaps you might give it a miss.

Further information

USEFUL WEBSITES

Apprenticeships	www.apprenticeships.org.uk
The Engineering Council	www.ecuk.org.uk
Connexions	www.connexions-direct.com
About Diplomas	www.ypdirect.gov.uk/diplomas
Edexcel	www.edexcel.org.uk
City & Guilds	www.cityandguilds.com

Sector Skills Councils

Automotive Engineering	www.automotiveskills.org.uk
Construction	www.constructionskills.com
Oil, Gas, Chemicals and Pharmaceuticals	www.cogent-ssc.org
Information Technology/ Telecommunications	www.e-skills.com
Energy, Water and Utilities	www.eu-skills.co.uk
Food and Drink	www.improveltd.co.uk
Environmental/Land	www.lantra.co.uk
Processing/Manufacturing	www.proskills.co.uk
Science and Engineering	www.semta.org.uk
Building Services	www.summitskills.org.uk

To employers and further education providers
Whether you want to be an architect (Construction and
the Built Environment Diploma); a graphic designer
(Creative and Media Diploma); an automotive engineer
(Engineering Diploma); or a games programmer (IT
Diploma), we've got a Diploma to suit you. By taking our
Diplomas you'll develop essential skills and gain insight
into a number of industries. Visit our website to see
the 17 different Diplomas that will be available to you.
www.diplomainfo.org.uk

AQA | City&
Guilds

PROFESSIONAL BODIES FOR ENGINEERING TECHNICIANS

Royal Aeronautical Society
4 Hamilton Place
London
W1V 0BQ
Tel: 020 7670 4300
www.aerosociety.com

Institution of Agricultural Engineers
Barton Road
Silsoe
Bedford
MK45 4FH
Tel: 01525 861096
www.iagre.org.uk

Chartered Institute of Building Services Engineers
Delta House
222 Balham High Road
London
SW12 9BS
Tel: 020 8675 5211
www.cibse.org.uk

Institute of Cast Metals Engineers
ICME Metalforming Centre
47 Birmingham Road
West Bromwich
B70 6PY
Tel: 0121 601 6979
www.icme.org.uk

Institution of Civil Engineers
1–7 Great George Street
London
SW1P 3AA
Tel: 020 7222 7722
www.ice.org.uk

Energy Institute
61 Cavendish Street
London
W1G 7AR
Tel: 020 7467 7100
www.energyinst.org.uk

Institute of Engineering & Technology
Michael Faraday House
Six Hills Way
Stevenage
SG1 2AY
Tel: 01438 313311
www.theiet.org.uk

Institution of Engineering Design
Courtleigh
Westbury Leigh
Westbury
BA13 3TA
Tel: 01373 822801
www.ied.org.uk

Society of Environmental Engineers
The Manor House
High Street
Buntingford
SG9 9PL
Tel: 01763 271209
www.environmental.org.uk

Institution of Fire Engineers
London Road
Moreton in Marsh
GL56 0RH
Tel: 01608 812580
www.ife.org.uk

Institution of Gas Engineers and Managers
Charnwood Wing
Ashley Road
Loughborough
LE11 3GH
Tel: 01509 282 728
www.igem.org.uk

Institution of Healthcare Engineering & Estate Management
2 Abingdon House
Cumberland Business Centre
Northumberland Road
Portsmouth
PO5 1DS
Tel: 023 9282 3186
www.iheem.org.uk

Institute of Highway Incorporated Engineers
De Morgan House
58 Russell Square
London
WC1B 4HS
Tel: 020 7436 7487
www.ihie.org.uk

Institution of Lighting Engineers
Regent House
Regent Place
Rugby
CV21 2PN
Tel: 01788 576492
www.ile.co.uk

Institute of Marine Engineering, Science and Technology
80 Coleman Street
London
EC2R 5BJ
Tel: 020 7382 2600
www.imarest.org.uk

Institute of Materials, Minerals and Mining
1 Carlton House Terrace
London
SW1Y 5DB
Tel: 020 7451 7300
www.iom3.org

Institute of Measurement and Control
87 Gower Street
London
WC1E 6AF
Tel: 020 7387 4949
www.instmc.org.uk

Institution of Mechanical Engineers
1 Birdcage Walk
London
SW1H 9JJ
Tel: 020 7222 7899
www.imeche.org.uk

Institute of the Motor Industry
Fanshaws
Brickendon
Hertford
SG13 8PQ
Tel: 01992 511521
www.motor.org.uk

Institution of Royal Engineers
Brompton Barracks
Chatham
ME4 4UG
Tel: 01634 822035
www.instre.org.uk

Royal Institute of Naval Architects
10 Upper Belgrave Street
London
SW1X 8BQ
Tel: 020 7235 4622
www.rina.org.uk

British Institute of Non-Destructive Testing
1 Spencer Street
Northampton
NN1 5AA
Tel: 01604 630124
www.bindt.org.uk

Institution of Nuclear Engineers
1 Penerley Road
London
SE6 2LQ
Tel: 020 8695 8220
www.bindt.org.uk

Society of Operations Engineers
22 Greencoat Place
London
SW1P 1PR
Tel: 020 7630 6666
www.soe.org.uk

Institute of Physics & Engineering in Medicine
Fairmount House
230 Tadcaster Road
York
YO24 1ES
Tel: 01904 610821
www.ipem.ac.uk

Institute of Plumbing & Heating Engineering
64 Station Lane
Hornchurch
RM12 6NB
Tel: 01708 472791
www.iphe.org.uk

Institution of Railway Signal Engineers
1 Birdcage Walk
London
SW1H 9JJ
Tel: 020 7808 1180
www.irse.org

Institution of Structural Engineers
11 Upper Belgrave Street
London
SW1X 8BH
Tel: 020 7235 4535
www.istructe.org.uk

Chartered Institution of Water & Environmental Managers
15 John Street
London
WC1N 2EB
Tel: 020 7831 3110
www.ciwem.org.uk

Institute of Water Officers
4 Carlton Court
Team Valley
Gateshead
NE11 0AZ
Tel: 0191 422 0088
www.iwo.org.uk

Welding Institute
Granta Park
Great Abington
Cambridge
CB1 6AL
Tel: 01223 891162
www.twi.co.uk